A Picture Book of
Jesse Owens

David A. Adler

illustrated by Robert Casilla

Holiday House/New York

For my brother Joe, who is always on the run

D.A.A.

For Little Robert and Carmen

R.C.

Text copyright © 1992 by David A. Adler
Illustrations copyright © 1992 by Robert Casilla
All rights reserved
Printed in the United States of America
First Edition

Library of Congress Cataloging-in-Publication Data
Adler, David A.
A picture book of Jesse Owens / David Adler : illustrated by
Robert Casilla.
p. cm.
Summary: A simple biography of the noted black track star who
competed in the 1936 Berlin Olympics.
ISBN 0-8234-0966-X
1. Owens, Jesse, 1913- —Pictorial works—Juvenile literatrue.
2. Track and field athletes—United States--Biography—Pictorial
works—Juvenile literature. [1. Owens, Jesse, 1913- . 2. Track
and field athletes. 3. Afro-Americans—Biography.] I. Casilla,
Robert, ill. II. Title.
GV697.09A651992   91-44735   CIP   AC
796.42'092—dc20
[b]

Jesse Owens was born on September 12, 1913, on a small farm in Oakville, Alabama. His given name was James Cleveland. His nickname was J.C.

J.C.'s grandparents had been slaves. His parents, Henry and Mary Emma Owens, were sharecroppers. They farmed on another man's land and shared with him their small crop of corn and cotton.

J.C.'s parents lived with their many children in a house that J.C. later described as "wooden planks thrown together." The roof leaked. In winter, cold wind blew through the walls. In summer, the house was so hot, J.C. felt he could hardly breathe.

J.C. was skinny and often sick with what his family called a "devil's cold." It was probably pneumonia. There was no money for doctors or medicine, so to cure J.C.'s illness, his mother wrapped him in cloth and put him by the fireplace.

A large lump once appeared on J.C.'s leg. His mother cut it out with a hot kitchen knife. J.C. said later that's when he learned "the meaning of pain."

When J.C. was about nine his family moved to what his mother said would be "a better life." They moved north to Cleveland, Ohio.

On J.C.'s first day of school in Cleveland, his teacher asked him his name. "J.C. Owens," he said. She thought he said "Jesse" and wrote that in her book. From then on he was known as Jesse Owens.

In Cleveland Jesse's father and older brothers worked in a steel mill. His mother worked washing clothes and cleaning houses. Jesse worked, too—sweeping floors, shining shoes, watering plants, and delivering groceries. Even with the whole family working, the Owenses were still very poor.

In 1927 Jesse entered Fairmount Junior High School. There he met Charles Riley, a gym teacher and coach of the track team. Riley saw Jesse run in gym class and asked him to train for the track team. Because Jesse worked afternoons, he met the coach every morning before school. Jesse felt very close to Coach Riley and called him "Pop."

Coach Riley taught Jesse to run as if the ground were on fire. He said Jesse should train not just for the next race, but to be the best runner he could be. He told Jesse to always train for the future—"for four years from next Friday."

With a lot of work and with what Jesse later called his "lucky legs," he ran so fast and with such grace that he was called a "floating wonder." One newspaper reporter wrote that when Jesse Owens ran, it seemed like he was about to "soar into the air."

In 1928 Jesse Owens set the junior high school record for the long jump and the high jump. In 1933 he set high school records for the long jump and for the 220-yard dash.

He went to Ohio State University and was on the track team there, too. On May 25, 1935, at the Big Ten Championship meet, Jesse had what has been called the greatest day in track-and-field history. He set three world records and tied a fourth, all within forty-five minutes.

Several weeks later, on July 5, 1935, Jesse Owens married Minnie Ruth Solomon, a young woman he had met at Fairmount Junior High School. He said later, "I fell in love with her the first time we talked, and a little more every time after that." She was quiet, smart, a loving and supportive wife for Jesse, and a good mother to their three daughters, Gloria, Marlene, and Beverly.

In 1936 the Olympic games were held in Berlin, Germany. Adolf Hitler, the German Nazi leader at the time, said native Germans were part of a "master race"; that blacks and especially Jews were inferior. Jesse Owens and other athletes proved he was wrong. Jesse Owens won four gold medals and was the hero of the 1936 Olympics.

He tied the Olympic record of 10.3 seconds for the 100-meter race, set a new world record of 20.7 seconds for 200 meters around a curve, and was part of the team to set a record for the 400-meter relays.

With a long jump of 26 feet, 5⁵⁄₁₆ inches (8.06 meters), Jesse Owens set a new Olympic record, too.

He "seemed to be jumping clear out of Germany," wrote one reporter.

Lutz Long, the popular German jumper who came in second, ran over to shake Jesse's hand. The picture of the two athletes—a black American and a white German in the midst of all the hate and prejudice around them—is one of the lasting images of the 1936 Olympics.

There was a parade in Cleveland to welcome Jesse Owens home, and in New York City, he rode at the head of a ticker-tape parade of the entire Olympic team. But there was prejudice, too, and Jesse said later that when he returned to the United States, "I couldn't ride in the front of the bus . . . I couldn't live where I wanted."

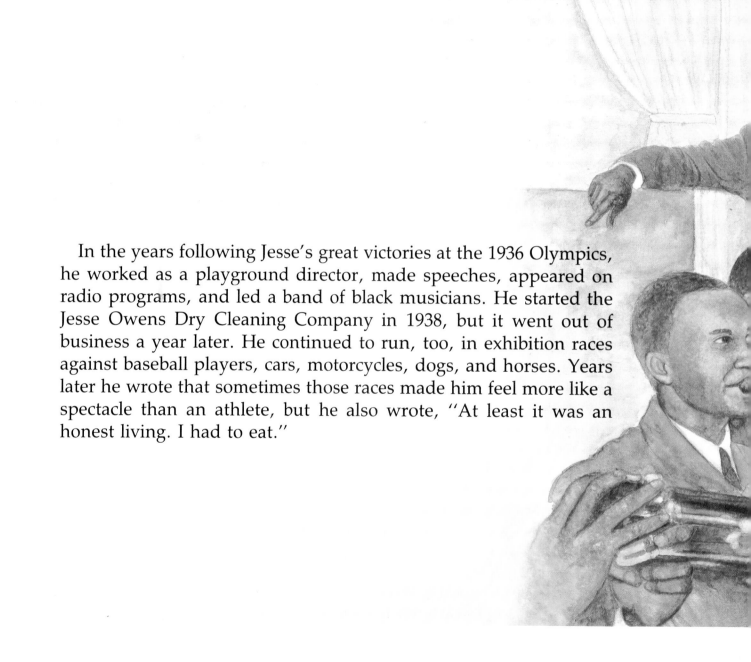

In the years following Jesse's great victories at the 1936 Olympics, he worked as a playground director, made speeches, appeared on radio programs, and led a band of black musicians. He started the Jesse Owens Dry Cleaning Company in 1938, but it went out of business a year later. He continued to run, too, in exhibition races against baseball players, cars, motorcycles, dogs, and horses. Years later he wrote that sometimes those races made him feel more like a spectacle than an athlete, but he also wrote, "At least it was an honest living. I had to eat."

Jesse Owens gave hundreds of speeches on the value of family, religion, and hard work. He was warm and friendly, and audiences loved to listen to him.

Jesse Owens also wrote his autobiography and two books on issues facing the black community. In the first one, *Blackthink: My Life as Black Man and White Man*, he wrote, "If the Negro doesn't succeed in today's America, it is because he has chosen to fail." Two years later, in *I Have Changed*, he seemed more aware of the prejudice blacks faced every day and showed more understanding for those who fought for equality.

For many years Jesse Owens was called the "World's Fastest Human," and he won many awards. In 1950 he was named the all-time greatest track-and-field athlete by the Associated Press. In 1976 President Gerald R. Ford gave him the Presidential Medal of Freedom. In 1979 President Jimmy Carter gave him the Living Legends Award.

Jesse Owens died of lung cancer on March 31, 1980, in Tucson, Arizona. People all over the world were saddened as they remembered his great victories and his warm smile. The races Jesse Owens ran were over in seconds, but the story of his rise from a poor sharecropper's son to a world hero has inspired young people to dream and to work hard to make their dreams come true.

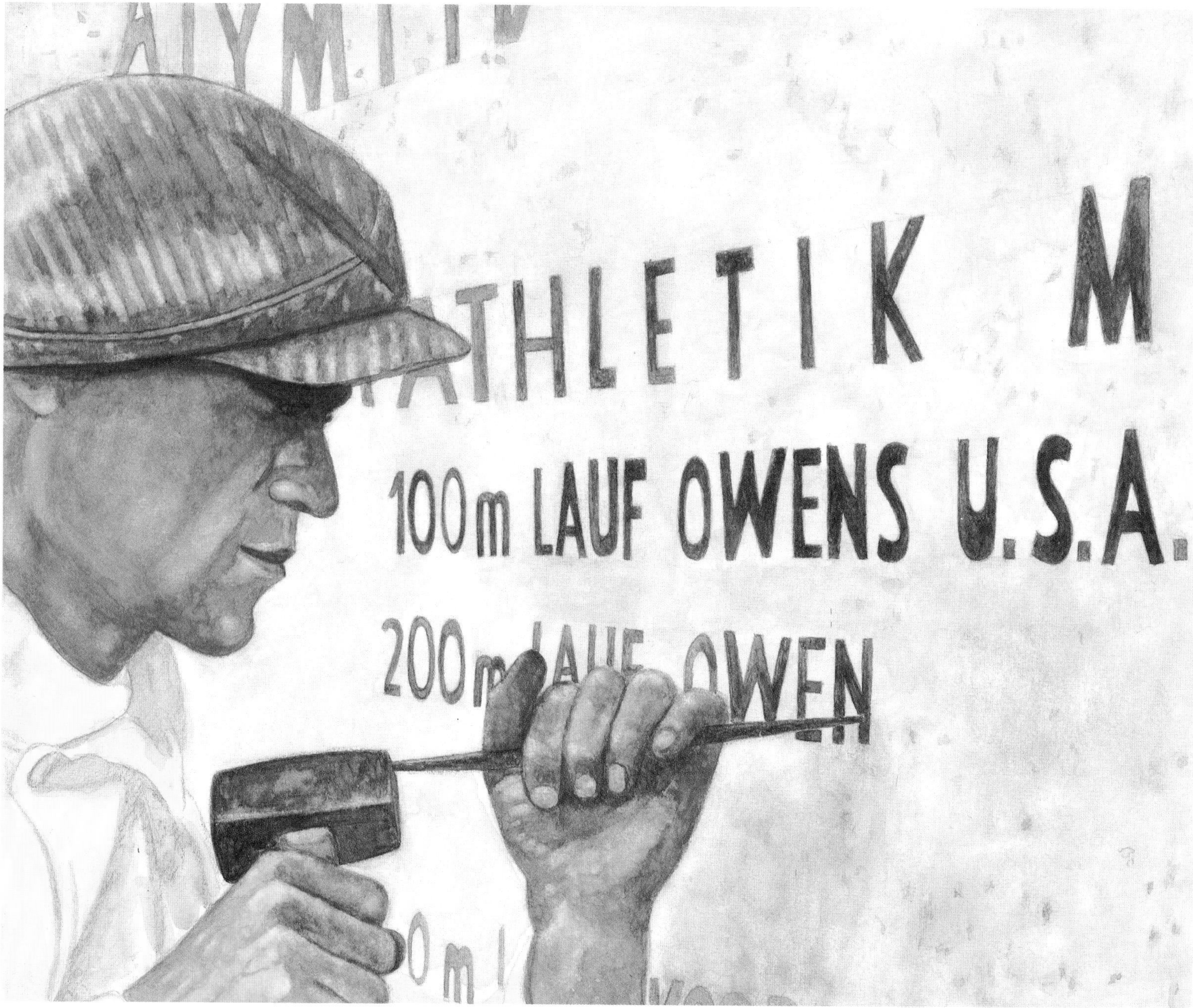
100m LAUF OWENS U.S.A.
OWEN

AUTHOR'S NOTES

When Jesse Owens competed, the long jump was called the broad jump.

There was a widely told story that Lutz Long gave Jesse Owens advice at the 1936 Olympics which helped him to qualify for the long jump; however, reporters at the games do not believe that Long and Owens spoke before Owens's winning jump.

On August 8, 1936, the day of the 400-meter relay race, the United States Olympic Committee pulled Sam Stoller and Marty Glickman, two Jewish runners, off the team. They were replaced by Jesse Owens and Ralph Metcalfe, both black. In 1936 there were many anti-Jewish laws in Germany. Many observers believed Stoller and Glickman were pulled from the team to save the Nazis the embarrassment of having them win gold medals.

Soon after Jesse Owens won his first medal, one newspaper wrote "Hitler Snubs Jesse." The story spread that Hitler congratulated other Olympic winners but would not shake hands with Jesse Owens because he was black. But the "snub" really came one day earlier. On the first day of the games, Hitler congratulated German and Finnish medal winners. But when Cornelius Johnson and David Albritton, black Americans, won gold and silver medals for the men's high jump, Hitler left the stadium. After that first day, he didn't invite any of the medal winners to his private area to congratulate them.

IMPORTANT DATES

1913 Born on September 12 in Oakville, Alabama.

1922 Moved to Cleveland, Ohio. (The exact year of the move is not known, but Jesse Owens often recalled it as being 1922.)

1927 Joined the track team at Fairmount Junior High School.

1935 Set three world records and tied a fourth at the Big Ten Championships in Ann Arbor, Michigan, on May 25.

1935 Married Minnie Ruth Solomon on July 5.

1936 Won four gold medals at the Olympic games in Berlin, Germany.

1950 Named the world's greatest track-and-field athlete by the Associated Press.

1970 His book, *Blackthink: My Life as Black Man and White Man*, was published.

1972 His book, *I have Changed*, was published.

1976 Awarded the Presidential Medal of Freedom by President Ford.

1979 Awarded the Living Legends Award by President Carter.

1980 Died in Tucson, Arizona, on March 31.

2